Lessons on Surrender from a Cowgirl and a King

Lisa Boucher

She Writes Press

Published 2022
Printed in the United States of America
Print ISBN: 978-1-64742-263-9
E-ISBN: 978-1-64742-264-6
Library of Congress Control Number: [LOCCN]

For information, address:
She Writes Press
1569 Solano Ave #546
Berkeley, CA 94707

She Writes Press is a division of SparkPoint Studio, LLC.

Names and identifying characteristics have been changed to protect the privacy of certain individuals.

To some of the best people I know, my twins and their spouses:

Austin and Alexis

Collin and Kiera

No matter what happens in your lives, stay in the saddle, and ride it out. Everything works out in the end. It always does.

Jeremiah 29:11

Contents

Introduction

We trek from birth to death, but it's *how* we travel along life's passageway that matters. As a fifteen-year-old, I took a particular horseback ride that etched itself into my memory. I couldn't have known then that it would later emerge as a metaphor for letting go, nor could I have discerned that decisive surrender is the pathway to peace.

The significance of that long-ago ride is now clear, but as a teen, I gleaned little insight from the experience. It was only when the memory resurfaced years later, around the same time that I read, yet again, the biblical story and prayer of King Jehoshaphat in 2 Chronicles, that I understood my task.

As most writers will attest, sometimes a story chooses you. I'm fascinated by the story of King Jehoshaphat, and when I wed it to my favorite childhood memory, the message becomes clear: We struggle because we hang on too tight. We want what we want, and it's only in the surrender that we will find peace. If we want tranquility, we have to let go!

We live in a complicated world. People are plagued by anxiety, depression, and fear. And what resides at the bottom of those uncomfortable emotions is the desire for control. We become anxious and fearful when we want things to go a certain way. We stand firm and exert our will because we are afraid of what could happen if we don't get our way. We want things to unfold as we think they should, and when they don't go as planned, we push harder. The problematic relationships and situations that torment us turn into granite slabs that will not budge. It is only when we let go, when we relinquish all self-will, that our struggles with anxiety, depression, and other emotional maladies cease to torment us.

I've journeyed down a few trails, some good and some not so good. A worthy trail ride, just like life, can be messy or hard to navigate, but in both living and riding, each day we're presented with new lessons—it's knowing how to tune in to the lessons that God wants to teach us that's the hard part.

Pray. Trust. Ride. encourages you to stay in the saddle and ride through life with a loose rein. We live more fully when we can let go—even when all looks bleak and our brains scream, *hang on and do something! Do anything! Fix this! Stop that!* The truth is, those problems that strangle our hearts are the sort of problems that we can't fix. Letting go allows us to accept that we'll have problems and people in our lives that we can love but that we can't control. We can't save others from themselves. We can't stop the inevitable from happening, but we can let go.

We hold on because of fear. It's the fear of the unknown that propels us to clutch the illusion that we have the power to alter outcomes. Anxiety lives in the future—that space and place where we travel in our minds and forget to take God with us. Living well is about keeping our wits; it's not about giving up on the dream, but about giving up on the way we think the dream should unfold. In all cases and phases of life, we can find our peace when we learn to rely more on God than we do our finite selves.

Letting go doesn't mean that we will live a problem-free life or that we must push people away. It's the way we think about our problems and those difficult people in our lives that determines whether or not we'll have peace. Consider a skittish horse who has had bad experiences with humans in the past. Its anxiety shows in obvious ways—it might prance, have a wild look in its eyes, or attempt to flee if restrained. The first instinct of a scared horse is to bolt. When you break a horse, it's natural for it to reject the bit, the saddle, and even the rider at first, but with patience, it will come to learn that battling what's in front of it produces more stress.

Can we control the river's current? Can we stop a loved one from getting ill or prevent any number of accidents or mishaps? Can we make great things happen or prevent bad things from happening? Can we stop the storms and the floods? Of course not! None of us has that sort of power or influence, and yet, how often do we fight for the illusion of control? Can we recognize that all forms of self-will are futile attempts to manipulate outcomes? Let's face it: micromanaging does nothing but leave us feeling more frustrated and exhausted than ever.

Within this book are vignettes and anecdotes to contemplate. Other pages might have a few words or a short thought aimed to snatch you out of an unconstructive thought pattern. Are you tired of struggling? Are you ready to get into the stream of life? If you answered yes, or even maybe, please keep reading. Of course, you'll have to do some steering and keep your eyes wide open to navigate around obstacles that may block the way, but as life goes on, you can let go and ask God for help.

We can choose to dodge the mindset that turns our problems into insurmountable hurdles that strangle our hearts and steal our joy. We get to choose whether we'll appreciate the journey or waste the whole ride because we're so caught up in fear and projection that we miss the scenery.

There's much to learn about life from the trail. Come, let's take a little ride.

Let Go of the Reins

One sticky summer evening in Hubbard, Ohio, I did just that—I let go of the reins. The year was 1975. I'd completed a long session at the 4-H barn and had a six-mile ride home. I knew the trail well as I'd traveled it twice a week for the past three years. I never tired of the landscape; nature always had something to give.

There was the area of conifers that dropped a carpet of needles for my horse to tread upon, then the stretch of trail flanked by wide-open fields, where Indian grass swayed in the breeze alongside Virginia wild rye, bergamot, and purple prairie clover. Next was the portion of the trail that snaked along a landowner's split-rail fence, the spaces between the splintered logs kissed with color from the black-eyed Susans, Queen Anne's lace, and purple asters, whose dutiful heads dipped and bobbed in the breeze and grew wild in every direction.

I loved riding in every season, but there was something special about October, when the surrounding woods turned ablaze—shades of gold, rust, and red, brilliant as any painted canvas. And so it went, the seasons on the trail, not unlike the seasons of our lives—each one distinct, but with the passage of time and phases blurred around the edges.

This particular day, my palomino quarter horse, Sham, plodded along without a care, and with the slightest pressure from one of my thighs, he responded and veered right. We'd reached the cutoff where we left a country road to traipse the well-worn path that sloped down to a small ditch and then up a short but steep bank, where we entered the pine grove, a space that in every season felt green and peaceful and smelled like Christmas. The pine grove spilled out to another field, where I slowed Sham to an even lazier walk. For a brief few weeks in July, when we'd pass the bramble patch, I'd lean down and pluck handfuls of wild blackberries, popping them into my mouth as fast as I could pick. Up ahead, a fair distance from the blackberry patch, was the part of the trail that was deep woods. The mix of deciduous and evergreen trees reminded me of people—some stood tall and proud while others looked splintered and frail, their sparse or dying leaves dangling from brittle branches, the weaker ones propped up by the strong until a rutting deer or a gust of wind knocked them down, and there they'd sleep until the earth that had given them birth swallowed them back up.

The wooded portion of the trail seemed to change from ride to ride: it was common to encounter low-slung branches, felled trees that blocked the path, and, in the dense shade after a soaking rain, patches of boggy mud that I'd look to avoid. The trail eventually opened up again into fields with the occasional sycamore tree, and then there was the home stretch—an old farm road no longer in use that wandered past apple, cottonwood, elm, maple, and oak trees, and the verdant pasture where, later, Sham might graze alongside Dunny and Lady, the two horses that lived next door.

Somewhere between the blackberry bushes and the

deep woods, the storm commenced—a deluge from the get-go. Sheets of water plunged from the sky. Veins of lightning ripped across the horizon, each bolt followed by clangs of sonorous thunder so vicious that I felt the vibration in my bones. I'd been caught in thunderstorms before, but this one was different. The lightning—nasty and nonstop—had my heart pounding. We needed shelter. Sham? He was none too pleased with the thudding clouds either.

When he started to prance, I choked up on the reins. He craned his neck and glanced back at me—the one eye that I caught in my vision and read well told me that he was about to come unglued. I didn't want him to get full-on spooked, so I did the only thing I could think to do, and that was to get moving. I gathered the reins and knotted the ends together—my hands were slippery from the water, and I couldn't risk a dropped strap. I looped the reins over the horn and stabilized them with slight pressure from my thumb. I jammed my heels down in the stirrups and sank deep in the saddle. I leaned low over Sham's withers, gave him his head, and with a perfunctory squeeze of my thighs let him fly.

Sham knew the trail as well as I did—I had to trust him. I had to trust that he'd see whatever obstacle he needed to see and would find a way to jump over or skirt past whatever he needed to dodge. I was of no help. Visibility from my vantage point was now zero as water pounded and stung my eyes.

Horse and rider moved as one. He jumped over fallen branches, snaked his way through the wooded trail, and navigated sharp turns at a fast canter. I rode slightly bent over the horn. There was no way for me to know if a low-slung branch would mar the way and knock me out of the saddle. I rode with prayers on my lips that the incessant lightning wouldn't strike us, and then I let go. There was no point in trying to steer. There was nothing I could do to assure our safety. We were in God's hands.

I've come to understand that that sort of letting go is how God wants us to live our lives. He wants us to trust him. He wants us to stop steering, plotting, or planning. He wants us to let go of the reins.

God wants us to stop deciding what we want to happen and forget all about what we think should happen and what direction we should go. He wants us to run to him and let him guide our course. Our part is to use our God-given intelligence to make the best decisions that we can, and then we must leave the results up to him. On that fateful ride in the storm, when I let go of the reins, I allowed providence to ride.

While still a ways out, I glimpsed the faint light coming from the barn, and I knew we were safe. We'd made it through the storm. God wants us to do that in our lives. He wants us to make it through every storm that life throws at us. It took me longer than I'd like to admit to realize that if I could trust my horse to deliver me home, surely I could trust God in all things big and small.

King Jehoshaphat

Perhaps you're familiar with King Jehoshaphat—the benevolent king of Judah? (If not, you can read about him in the appendix.)

"Jehoshaphat was frightened, and he hastened to consult the Lord" (2 Chronicles 20:3). The king knew that he and his people couldn't withstand an attack. Three armies were headed toward them; the Moabites, Ammonites, and Meunites were on the march from Edom to invade Judah. King Jehoshaphat had little time to gather an army or formulate a plan against the encroaching enemies. He was desperate and out of options.

Who among us hasn't felt out of options? Who hasn't at some point felt hopeless or crushed by the weight of their circumstances? It's part of plodding along life's trail—we can expect moments or periods in life when anxiety spikes and faith runs low.

Yet no matter how we feel, it helps to realize that feelings aren't fact. Just because we *feel* a certain way about a given situation doesn't mean that situation *is* the way we feel about it. Feelings and emotions are full of trickery. We may be convinced that things are a certain way, but when we step back and gain a new perspective, reality looks a bit different, and it can look especially different to the person standing on the other side of the stream. The fastest way to cloud our judgment is to stay locked in our own heads. We can fall into the trap of myopic vision, and from that restricted vantage point, we can believe that circumstances and the people around us are only as we see them.

Hope abounds when we learn to get out of our own way. Hope flourishes when we sear it into our brains and live in the firm knowledge that God's ways are not our ways and his perspective is not our perspective. God does not think the way we do or solve problems the way we do. The Bible tells us that the mind of God is different than the minds of humans, yet too often we try to humanize God and wonder why things are the way that they are or we resent that he doesn't do things the way we think they should be done:

> *For my thoughts are not your thoughts,*
> *nor are your ways my ways, says the Lord.*
> *As high as the heavens are above the earth,*
> *so high are my ways above your ways*
> *And my thoughts above your thoughts.*
> (Isaiah 55:8–9)

Yet how often do we decide that God does not care and that God is not helping us because our preferred results haven't manifested? When we accept God's divinity and our limited insight and abilities, well, that place of acceptance can be a jumping-off point to learn a new way of thinking and living.

We find peace when we can let go and stop ruminating and projecting. We find peace when we learn to detach from others—when we can accept that they have their lessons and it is not our place to fix them or avert life from happening to them. When we can accept that God deals with each one of us individually and throws situations, consequences, and lessons in our path so that we learn what God wants us to learn, we'll feel less anxious. Once we accept God's sovereignty, we can let go with confidence.

It may seem counterintuitive to let go and stop controlling, but the alternative is to live with unchecked anxiety. Letting go feels uncomfortable because for most, it's an unpracticed ability. It's like getting on a horse. The first few times you ride can feel sort of scary, but once you figure out how to use the reins and you make friends with your mount, there's a feeling of freedom.

In order to learn any new behavior or skill, we must accept that there will be discomfort. Most new riders have sore legs the first few times they ride a horse because they're exercising a whole new set of muscles. The same goes with our behaviors. If we're not uncomfortable, then we're not practicing anything new; we're stuck in old behaviors, old patterns.

If we want to adopt new behaviors and ways of

thinking, we have to practice. We can start by stopping ourselves from rehearsing what-ifs. We can stop rehashing conversations in our heads. When we let go and no longer rail against reality, our pain lessens. People suffer when they wrestle against themselves, when the status quo is too painful. The internal angst becomes so uncomfortable, even debilitating, that the desire is to flee, self-medicate, or change the external circumstances and dynamics so that internally we can feel better.

We have to be okay on the inside regardless of what is happening around us. The things in life that we combat the most are those things that are out of our realm of control, yet we fight them anyway.

What if we stopped battling people and situations? What if we stopped attempting to manipulate outcomes? What if, instead of struggling, we changed our thoughts and practiced faith-filled actions? We could pray; hand the matter over to God and let him figure it out; be still; wait; do nothing. The choice to not take an action is in itself an action.

The above suggestions may seem counterintuitive

because they require us to choose alternative actions, but small changes in our thinking and daily life can add up to huge results where peace is the prize.

King Jehoshaphat took an action that at the time must have seemed contradictory to what a king would normally do—after all, aren't kings supposed to have a plan or know what to do to protect their people? King Jehoshaphat appeared to be helpless because he didn't have a battle plan, but he had a prayer plan. He gathered his people in the assembly of Judah and Jerusalem and prayed, "O our God, will you not pass judgment on them? We are powerless before this vast multitude that comes against us. We are at a loss what to do, hence our eyes are turned toward you" (2 Chronicles 20:12).

To some of the people, King Jehoshaphat's reaction might have seemed foolish. What sort of a king has no plan but a prayer? His actions may have felt inadequate, but he had no better choice.

We will never know all King Jehoshaphat's thoughts, but we know that he was scared. Scripture tells us,

"Jehoshaphat was frightened, and he hastened to consult the Lord. He proclaimed a fast for all of Judah" (2 Chronicles 20:3).

He did what he knew he could do, but then he let go and trusted God. He gave it all up to heaven and prayed, "Lord, God of our fathers, are you not the God in heaven, and do you not rule over all the kingdoms of the nations? In your hand is power and might, and no one can withstand you" (2 Chronicles 20:6).

Read that last line again: "In your hand is power and might, and no one can withstand you." What a comforting phrase. But do you believe it? Do you practice it in your own life?

You can say you believe, but if you don't practice faith and flex your faith muscles, then you're talking the talk but not walking the walk. Do you believe God is large and in charge? If you believe that God is in control, then act like it and ask yourself, "Why am I so anxious? Angry? Disappointed? Why am I scared?"

Jehoshaphat prayed. He admitted his powerlessness. He knew he could do nothing against the multitude that advanced against him and his people. He knew he had one way out of his predicament, and that was to let go and trust God.

How many times have you felt powerless over the circumstances in your life? The spouse who dies or leaves, unforeseen physical illnesses, mental health illnesses, job woes, financial stressors, addiction . . . there are a plethora of things that happen in life that matter a great deal, but over most of them, you have no control. Once you can let that fact seep into your bones, you'll begin to let go of anxiety, of the need to know, of the need to have it your way, of the need to control situations in order to lock in outcomes that make you feel comfortable and secure.

Fear dwells at the base of anxiety. Understand that you may have to accept an outcome that you find unacceptable—it's that juncture of reluctant tolerance and agreement that allows you to let go.

Often I find that my thoughts can flit off in all sorts of directions. If I allow my mind to wander, I can project and conjure up all sorts of scenarios that might happen—but most likely they won't happen. Over the years I've retrained my brain by practicing faith. Nowadays, I don't spend too much time worrying about uncertainties and things that I can't control.

Such was the case when I got a call at two in the morning from my son's now wife, Kiera. She had called to let my husband and me know that, as we spoke, our son was lying on a gurney and was being wheeled into the operating room at a hospital in Michigan. She went on to say that he had smashed his arm against a boat the day before and he had compartment syndrome.

Compartment syndrome is a serious condition where the muscles swell and bleed from within as a result of blunt-force trauma; if surgery isn't done immediately, permanent nerve or muscle damage can result. In some cases, patients can lose limbs.

Any call received at two o'clock in the morning is most likely not good news. As I picked up my phone, a text came through on my husband's cell, and our other son called the landline. The conversation with Kiera, went like this:

"Hi, Lisa, I thought I better let you know your son is going into surgery now."

"What! What happened?"

"He was in the Poconos and hit his arm."

"What do you mean he hit his arm?"

"On a boat. They said he has compartment syndrome."

"Who's doing the surgery?"

"I'm not sure."

"Do they know what they're doing? Are they any good?"

"I don't know."

"How long are they going to keep him there?"

"I don't know."

I realized that any more questions would be answered the same way since she had just arrived. I asked for and jotted down the name of the hospital. I told Kiera that I was glad she was able to get to the hospital, that I appreciated that she was there with him, and that in the morning I'd head their way. There was nothing I could do at that moment, so I said a prayer, went back to bed, and slept fitfully. When I got up early the next morning to make the four-hour trip to Michigan, my husband couldn't believe it. He said he'd been up all night, and he seemed almost annoyed that I'd fallen back to sleep.

I asked him what good it would have done for me to stay up all night and worry. When we can't control what's happening or do anything about a specific situation, that is precisely when we need to let go and give it to God. If I had stayed up all night fretting, I would've been exhausted in the morning, and that would've made the drive to Michigan all the more difficult.

By the time I got to Michigan, my son was out of surgery. His arm was saved, and with rehab, full function would be restored, though he'd have a wicked scar from his palm to his deltoid.

There will be many times in our lives when we'll only find peace if we learn to trust God and put the whole situation in his lap. This is as true now as it was for King Jehoshaphat. In the assembly of Judah and Jerusalem, a Levite named Jahaziel was struck by the spirit of God. He told the people of Judah, "Do not fear or lose heart at the sight of this vast multitude, for the battle is not yours but God's" (2 Chronicles 20:15).

That's right. Life isn't our battle to endure; it's God's. He will endure for us if we let him, but as long as we're trying to control every last aspect of our lives, we cannot know peace. However, when we let go, we can see and experience God's providence.

The Rattlesnake and the Meadowlark

My adult life landed me in the suburbs. I made that choice, but there were times when I felt claustrophobic due to the lack of open space. I sometimes wondered how a country girl ended up in a place where strip malls and fast-food outlets were more plentiful than animals.

I had a dog, but I missed being around horses. There's just something about a horse—once you've bonded with one, their essence seeps into your blood. I particularly appreciated the few short years that I had lived in Texas. At the time, equine and cattle themes permeated every aspect of everyday life in the Lone Star State, and there, I felt at home.

In my adult life, riding hadn't remained in the

forefront, but there was no way I was going to give it up altogether. I found several working ranches in Wyoming that allowed me to relive what I think were some of my best days as a child and then a teenager—the days I spent on the back of my horse.

I located places that weren't dude ranches. I didn't want touristy gimmicks. I wanted to ride. Outside of Pinedale, Wyoming, I found a real working ranch that a few times a year took on guests to help a coalition of ranchers move their cattle.

When you're eight thousand feet up the mountain and you look around and see nature spilling its beauty in every direction, it's hard not to be in awe of our world—unless, of course, you're focused on snakes.

This time, I was in Cody, Wyoming, on what was called the Sedona Ride. It was one of those trails where I could've easily thought I was in Arizona instead of Wyoming. The russet-colored dirt; the red hills and plateaus; the rugged beauty of rocky trails dotted with Indian paintbrush and yellow rabbitbrush—the simple beauty of the rusty landscape enchanted me. And the environs were silent as a painting—all except for the rattlesnakes.

In all that beauty I thought I'd be able to remain wholly present in the moment, but I have to tell you, that wasn't the case. My thoughts drifted to what was below me. It wasn't the warm breeze or the red hills that I noticed; rather, it was the prairie rattlesnakes slinking through the brush and darting across the trail that gripped my attention.

That particular day, I rode with two or three other people, and the wrangler might have mentioned something about the snakes. Otherwise, he seemed unfazed by the numerous reptiles that slunk through the brush. I, on the other hand, was obsessed with wanting the rattlers to go away.

We rode through open fields and up a rocky slope to an area known as the Chugwater formation: a large swath of land that extends north of Wyoming into Montana and south into Colorado. The formation is made up of layers of sandstone, siltstone, and gypsum, depending on where exactly you are—but it was in this area where the snakes were plentiful. So numerous were the prairie rattlers that when we quieted our horses, you could hear rattling as they slid through the dirt.

I couldn't help but imagine all sorts of horrible things that might happen if I fell off the horse. I'm terrified of snakes, poisonous or not—I prefer not to see them or even think about them. But here I was riding along as they glided among the rocks, grasses, and dirt. All I kept thinking was, *What if I fall off this horse?* Never mind that this was an irrational fear—I've been riding since I was five years old, and I was confident in my riding abilities. In addition, my mount, Emma, was all too familiar with not only the terrain but also the flora and fauna. It was unlikely that something as small as a snake would cause her to spook.

And so, while I rode against a backdrop of red hills, cobalt sky, and silvery sagebrush, the clear song of the western meadowlark pulled me back to the present. Except for its yellow belly and throat, this otherwise unpretentious bird sings a melodious song, pure and clear. I brought Emma to a halt to hunt for the source of the melody, and there, perched on a sage twig, the lowly bird sang its little heart out as it swayed in the breeze.

We'd stopped for a good five minutes, and then one of the wranglers pointed to the trail that sloped left. He and the others disappeared around the bend. I gathered my reins to keep up. As we loped through the meadow, I decided that I loved everything about the moment except the snakes. And then it hit me—why in all that beauty and bliss did I keep going back to the snakes?

Was it just me? Or is it part of the human condition that keeps us focusing on what we don't have or on what is wrong or missing from our lives or our experiences, instead of focusing on all that is good and right? Why is it easier to project and think negative thoughts than it is to dwell in the present moment and think good thoughts? Why is it difficult to default to gratitude when there is so much to be grateful for? If we're not careful with our thoughts, even when we're steeped in beauty, we can summon up ashes.

Our thoughts create emotion. Will we think good thoughts and have good emotions, or will we think fearful thoughts and breed anxiety? Which one is it going to be?

God tells us, "Do not fear or lose heart" (2 Chronicles 20:15). God also tells us to focus on what is good. Through Paul, He says, "Finally, brothers, whatever is true, whatever is honorable, whatever is just, whatever is pure, whatever is lovely, whatever is gracious, if there is any excellence and if there is anything worthy of praise, think about these things" (Philippians 4:8–9).

Forty minutes into the ride, I flipped the switch. I decided that I needed to let go of any more thoughts about the snakes. Instead, I'd enjoy the moment. I turned my attention to the buttery leather of my chaps and how soft they felt against my fingertips. I focused on the sound of gravel crunching beneath Emma's hooves. I expressed gratitude for the moment and for Emma. She was a sturdy mare who did an excellent job navigating rocks, boulders, and gopher holes. She traversed steep hills and valleys with aplomb, and everything under the sun was glorious.

When I changed the tone of my thoughts, both my external and internal world changed as well.

Let Go

If you want divine help, you have to ask. Once you've made the request, take a step back and let God do his work. God will not interfere in our free will. I used to hold on to people, places, and things and allow myself to get beat up emotionally and spiritually before I let go—but that has all changed. I no longer want to hold on to things that hurt. The easier, softer way to live is to let go. Once you make the choice to hand over all of your problems to God, you'll come to relish the rest that comes with surrender.

Holding on burns energy. Think of the emotional capital it takes to plot, plan, and micromanage the minutiae of your life. Are you done being weary?

Trusting God allows you to save your energy for the people and things that matter. You'll free up vast amounts of mental, emotional, and creative capital that you can direct to other people or things that interest you. Once you experience the freedom of detachment, a whole new interior life unfolds. You'll discover what it's like to have inner assets available to spend on things that inspire you. You will feel free when you no longer waste resources trying to control the uncontrollable. It's like a savings plan for energy. Instead of squandering your limited share on fretting, you can cash in on the discovery of new hobbies and talents that will emerge now that you've created space in your life for new things. You will experience emotional peace.

The people in Judah knew this. Nowhere in scripture does it say that they stayed up all night to worry and vex. Rather, they prayed, "We are at a loss what to do, hence our eyes are turned toward you" (2 Chronicles 20:12).

Turn to God and choose peace. Remember, the only thing that stands between peace and turmoil is the eighteen inches between your head and your heart.

See Me. Hear Me.

We search and search, yet all along we are looking for ourselves. Everyone wants to know that they matter, that they have significance, that they are not invisible. It takes a short minute to connect: Eye contact. A kind word. It's not difficult to let others know that you see them.

This is what we want. We want to be seen. We want to be heard.

Cowgirl Way

Do you have a code of ethics? Does your blueprint for life keep you in the track that feels right and good and true? Can you honor your core beliefs and defend them not because they're popular or part of any groupthink but because they're beliefs that matter to you? If you can make a concerted effort to define and live by your values, chances are slim that you'll fall prey to the endless changing tides found in our fickle culture.

King Jehoshaphat understood that we can follow a path of our choosing, and he chose to follow the path of his father, Asa, who was an honorable man: "He followed the path of his father Asa unswervingly, doing what was right in the Lord's sight" (Chronicles 20:32).

We can choose to follow God, or we can follow the world. Knowing where you stand allows you to navigate through life with a vision. If we lack a vision, we risk falling under the spell of all the worldly voices murmuring in our ears—the voices of strangers on social media, movies, and television, to name a few. Daily, we're bombarded by messages to eat this, drink that, gamble here, travel there, buy this, do that . . . instead, toss aside all worldly suggestions and blaze your own trail.

Attention

Pay attention to the people God puts in your life. Pay attention to the people God removes from your life, and when he does so, let them go!

More on Truth

When we speak the truth and stick to our truths, we come to know and respect ourselves. Without truth, self-respect and respect from others flees.

The ability to lie to others reinforces our ability to lie to ourselves, and in the end, no one wins.

Cowgirl Up

- Let go: Refuse to worry about the things that can't be changed. Let go of everything that is out of your control.
- Let go of any negative voices in your head that bring discouragement—reprogram your thoughts by refusing to focus on all that's bad in your life, and live in gratitude for all that's good.
- Talk to God. Every day do something to enlarge your spiritual life.
- Encourage someone else.
- Don't compromise who you are in order to fit in with others.

- Don't compare yourself to others. Comparisons breed unhappiness. Most comparisons make a person feel less than or superior but not equal.

- Don't lie. No embellishing allowed. If the truth isn't a good enough story, then maybe that story doesn't need to be told.

- Waste no time on people who don't respect your boundaries or appreciate your company. Learn to walk away—sooner rather than later.

- Choose to remove yourself and your energy from the people and battles that aren't yours to fight.

- Not everything or everyone deserves your time or your attention.

- Guard your heart, your energy, and your emotions. Lean away from those who don't respect your truth.

- If you follow the herd, you never get to lead. Be your own person.

- Face your fears.

- Have at least one animal friend.
- Live and love with those who allow a loose rein.
- Keep going and keep trying, but be willing to make a U-turn when it makes sense to do so.
- Don't get caught in your own web.
- Vow to never be the person who is all hat and no cattle—substance matters.

As I previously mentioned, I loved everything about Texas. It seemed no matter where I went, I'd run into an interesting character who had something to say. I was at the stockyards when I first overheard the expression "all hat and no cattle."

The man who said it looked to be out of central casting. His weathered face told me he could've been anywhere between sixty and eighty. He wore overalls and dusty boots, and he sucked on a blade of grass. He leaned on a rail as he waited for the upcoming auction. To the young man standing beside him, I heard him say, "Naw, don't bother with them people. They're all hat and no cattle."

I'm not sure who "them people" were, but the sentiment stuck.

Why should any of us waste time on people who are insincere or duplicitous? A horse can sense people and their motives. If a horse dislikes your energy, well, it might buck you right off its back.

How many times has someone made you false promises? Everyone has experienced disappointment. People say all sorts of things that they have no intention of doing. Parents do this sometimes just to quiet their kids, but why take the sloppy path instead of doing what's right?

Perhaps it's easier to tell people what they *want* to hear rather than tell them the truth.

Are we so uncomfortable that we might hurt someone's feelings or so convinced that we don't have the energy to engage in a real way that we'd rather lie instead? When we become comfortable lying about small things, lying about big things comes next.

You need a code. You need to know what you will compromise and where that trail ends.

Jealousy

Nothing kills a soul and dims your internal light faster than jealousy. Things in the natural world don't operate with an ounce of covetousness. Animals and plants are authentic. They experience life and accept their lives with dignity.

Can you imagine a daisy wanting to rip itself out of the garden because it would rather be a rose?

The natural world teaches us to be happy where we are. Each tree, each blade of grass, each animal or insect is perfectly content to be what God made it to be.

Strive to honor your whole self—to let go of who you think others want you to be. Stop wanting to be anyone but who you are, and focus instead on living your best life with dignity and grace.

Dark Nights

At some point in all of our lives, we can fall behind as easily as surge forward. Winners are made in the in-between spaces. It's how we trudge the mountain that matters, not just that we reach the summit.

King Jehoshaphat stayed true to himself, even when he was in a terrible predicament and his people were about to be crushed by moving armies. He was a man of God, and he did what a godly man would do when faced with a dire situation—he prayed. And God said, "Well done," because he and his people were saved. God saved the king and his people; he will save you too.

Cowgirl Wisdom

Find your happy place and go there often.

I've traveled to some cool places in my life, but my favorite place in all the world is in a barn, preferably a barn at dawn when the first rays of light pour through the open doors. I love the dust bunnies that dance in the sunlight, the low nickers of the horses, the clomp of hooves anxious for breakfast, the smell of hay and manure, the purr of a tabby as it unfurls itself from its bed of straw.

Everyone has a special place that makes them feel whole. Is it a favorite childhood memory that you can recreate? Is it a room in your house or apartment that makes you feel cocooned? Is it a specific location where you traveled? Is it outdoors? Whatever space or place it is that you love, try to spend time there. Your soul will thank you.

Nature Is Good Medicine

Nature is a teacher and a healer, but we can't learn or heal if we don't step outdoors. There is much to gather from the rocks, the trees, and the wildlife. Pay attention. The earth speaks to all who listen.

Journey to Self-Love

If you don't want to walk around wounded, you're responsible for pursuing the healing of your wounds. When you find the courage to heal, you find the courage to be who God intended you to be.

Gather your courage. Do the inside work. If necessary, seek professional help. Decide right now that staying stuck is not an option. Work to let go of the things that eat you up inside. When you heal your wounds, you'll find yourself. Those wounds have defined you far too long. Let them go.

Giddyup

Limit your time with toxic people—or better yet, take the cowgirl way and get on your horse and ride right out of their lives. Problem solved.

Meditation

Learn to meditate. It calms the mind and soothes the soul.

Priorities

The world will clamor for your attention. It will spar to yank you out of a place of peace. But when you have your priorities in place, you can wrench yourself back from the brink. Reject the world. Plant yourself in the presence of God—for there, under his mantle, is the good life.

Self-Forgiveness

If you try to move forward while looking back over your shoulder, you're bound to stumble.

Yes, wrong turns were taken and bad decisions were made, but the past is behind you now.

If you can forgive others, you can forgive yourself. Decide right now that you will think of it no more. You did the best you could at the time. Let the past remain the past. Move forward. Let it go!

Loss or Letting Go?

Not all losses are negative. We can look at the world as though every change is a loss, or we can look at each new change as an opportunity for growth, discovery, and freedom.

Life is about our soul's evolution. Some loss is necessary so that we can make room in our lives to embrace new things.

Free Will

Stop fighting God's omnipotence. Some people struggle to believe in God. Some reject the notion that God loves them. Could your disbelief in God have anything to do with crushing disappointments or hurts from the past?

Do you believe that God allowed terrible things to happen to you or a loved one, and you're angry that you weren't spared the agony of your experience? It's life's harsh circumstances and the obsession or disappointment with religion that causes people to turn their backs on God. Man does all the damage, yet we blame God.

Man has free will, and free will can lead to evil behaviors. Evil actions are not God's will. He didn't cause bad things to happen, but he'll give you the strength to get through them.

We're equipped to know God, but we aren't wired to seek God. That has to come from within. Whether we want to admit it or not, we need God. All of life's problems can be solved with a spiritual solution. As we saw with the story and prayer of King Jehoshaphat, our humanness has limits—but God has a solution.

Miracles

A changed heart is a miracle. It makes no difference if the change of heart happens to a human or a horse—the change occurs when a person or animal is reborn and renewed through love and through love only.

I've seen it over and over again in people who get sober. I've seen it over and over again in animals that were once angry and mean because they had been mistreated or abused but then learned to trust again. Something inexplicable transcends and transforms the heart, and that is love. God is love.

When you see an angry, bitter person let go of decades of resentments and their anger is replaced with love; when a person changes from being self-centered to other-centered; when you hear of incredible healings or how someone narrowly escaped death and there's no plausible explanation for how they survived—those are all miracles. Miracles abound, but if we don't believe that miracles are possible, we'll never see them.

The miracle of our senses is one gift that comes to mind. When we wake up each day, are we grateful enough? Do we appreciate that we can see? That we can hear? That we can sense the lightest of touches? Our senses are all extraordinary gifts, yet if you're like me, most times I take them for granted. I go about life assuming they will always be there, but the reality of living in an unsure world is that none of us has a guarantee of what tomorrow will bring.

Look into the eyes of a small child, and you'll see pure love and joy. To them, the world is a wondrous place. Their innocence is a blessing and a gift to remind us that we all start out innocent—it's the hardship of living in a cynical world that taints us.

How do the sun and the moon know what to do? How do the seasons know when to come and go? There is repetition in all of it, and yet in the middle of the mundane is the brilliance of order that brings forth the unending cycle of life, death, and rebirth.

As we grow spiritually, our attitudes and beliefs about the world evolve. We no longer have to allow the world and all its problems to overwhelm us. We can instead ask God to renew our hearts and to change our perspectives.

We

We are the answer to each other's problems. I learned from you, and now I can apply the same spiritual and practical principles to my life. Together we succeed.

Peace Is an Inside Job

We can be deeply flawed and still be deeply loved. We don't need to be perfect in order to be lovable. We are all imperfect. We are all worthy of love.

As we lean in and let go of the external things that we can't control, we also can strive to let go of the thorns in our inner chambers, those things that poke us from the inside out: guilt, shame, feelings of unworthiness, the pressure to be perfect . . .

Release all negative self-talk and internal musings that tell you that you're not good enough. Decide here and now to shred those destructive tapes. When a negative thought comes to mind, replace it with a favorite affirmation or scripture. Try this one: "I keep the Lord always before me; with the Lord at my right, I shall never be shaken" (Psalm 16:8).

You're Here

You can't be perfect, but you can be present. It takes discipline to pull our minds back to the here and now. Each moment is unique and cannot be relived.

We have the choice to appreciate the here and now, ruin it, or miss it altogether. Where are your feet? Here. Right here.

Relish this instant, for this is your life.

Enlightenment

God fully accepts you as you are, yet you struggle to feel worthy. Try not to "should" yourself. It takes effort to change tired thinking patterns and habits. It takes courage to look at your faults. It takes willingness to transform yourself into the person God intended you to be.

If you're willing to look at yourself, you're in wide-open territory. Ask God to show you the truth. Your day of enlightenment will come.

Ride On

If you want emotional growth, skip the shortcuts. Whatever hard thing is in front of you, face it, deal with it, and then accept it. The only way to get to the other side of any challenge is to plod through, no matter how much it hurts or how hard it may look. You gain nothing by avoiding a test. You're sturdier than you think.

Such was the case during my stay at the Box R Ranch, where I had to dig deep and cowgirl-up.

The coalition of ranchers in the area used to number twenty-five but had dwindled to nine. The remaining ranchers in the alliance needed all of the help they could get to move their cattle. The night before the cattle drive, the lead wrangler explained the logistics—the ranchers would all come from different directions. Once in the valley, the herds would converge into one huge herd, and all available hands would continue to move the cattle to a predesignated holding field. There, the cattle would rest for a day or two, which would allow the calves to mother-up, and then their fate was probably the nearest auction.

The wrangler made a point to say it'd be a long, hard day, and anyone not up for a twelve-hour day in the saddle had best stay back.

I crawled out of bed at three a.m. The cabin was warm and cozy, but the howling wind lured me to investigate outside. I cracked open the door and was met with a blast of arctic air. Big slushy snowflakes round as Ping-Pong balls plunged from the sky. Holy Moses—I didn't expect snow. It was June!

I slammed the door. Darn. It crossed my mind to crawl back in bed and say the heck with the cattle drive—but then again, I'd come to Wyoming for an adventure, so I knew I'd better get moving. I splashed water on my face and brushed my teeth. I pulled on long underwear, layered a wool sweater over a long-sleeved tee, grabbed my oilskin duster, and at the last minute thought to grab an extra pair of socks.

When I got to the corral, JR, the well-built Pinto I'd been riding the last five days, was nowhere in sight. Perhaps someone had loaded him in the trailer, I thought—but most of the other horses weren't even saddled yet. What was going on?

Above the blustering wind, I hollered, "Where's my horse?"

One of the wranglers, tall and lanky with a shock of blond hair that concealed most of his eyes, glanced my way. A sheepish grin played across his lips.

From the other side of the corral, I heard hooting and hollering. "Yeehaw! I told you. Give me my ten bucks!"

Apparently, a few of the wranglers had placed a bet on whether or not Mrs. Suburbia had enough moxie to get up before the break of dawn and brave the elements of what promised to be a grueling day.

We piled into the truck and set out with the horses in tow. Forty minutes later, the driver pulled into a flat grassy area off the highway. This was the starting point.

One of the wranglers would drive the trailer to the other side of the mountain and wait for our return there, sometime before dark.

We'd been in the saddle for about fifteen minutes when I caught a glimpse of movement down below. A rancher, riding at a fast trot, moved his herd through the valley. He worked the cattle with the help of three border collies. The way those dogs knew just what to do by following the rancher's hand signals was a sight to behold.

I expected the day to be a challenge, but it was the bone-chilling cold that bothered me the most, especially in my feet. Oh, and though I'd brought the extra socks, there was no time to stop. I should've just put them on when I had the chance.

We rode along a high ridge until we got to where we could move toward the valley along a traversing path. We passed the rancher, and he signaled for us to keep going. He and the dogs had his herd under control. We caught up with a few of the other ranchers who had much larger herds that were converging, and they needed assistance.

A handful of cows splintered off and scattered. Within minutes, we rounded up the strays and had all the cows moving in the direction they were meant to go.

At the top of a smaller ridge, I snapped to attention at the unmistakable sound of rushing water. From my vantage point on the hill, I scrutinized the parade of cattle as they slogged through the river. I surmised that in certain spots it was deeper than expected. Some of the calves were up to their necks in water, and a few of the smaller ones struggled to cross. It occurred to me that between the steep slope down and the steep incline up the other side of the bank, this crossing could get tricky. Would my stirrups clear the water? Sure, I had an extra pair of socks, but riding for the next ten hours in wet boots wasn't an option I wanted to consider. I couldn't take my feet out of the stirrups because I'd need them to navigate the steep descent and incline on the other side.

I had no other choice. I'd have to ride through the swift-moving river whether I wanted to or not, and if I got wet, so be it.

JR descended the bank, sliding in spots where the grass had been stripped down to mud by all of the hooves. His broad chest and sturdy hindquarters enabled him to plow through the rushing current like a champ. The messy part for both of us was when he tried to exit the river. Because of the hundreds of cattle that had already crossed, the edge of the riverbank looked like quicksand. JR struggled to find his footing. I gave him his head and all the rein he needed to lift himself out of the muck and get us both up the bank.

Much to my dismay, it was impossible not to get wet, and once we stood on solid ground again, I realized I was soaked up to my knees.

The whole experience mirrored life. There are times when we have no other choice but to move through situations with grit. We might get dirty. We might suffer. We might struggle. The reality of life on the trail is that things can get dicey and messy, and our lives off the trail will too. But no matter what it is that we have to get through, we can turn to God, like King Jehoshaphat did, and have faith that we can and will come out of our troubles. It might get a little messier than we thought it would, but we'll be stronger, wiser, and, with God's grace, more steadfast in our faith.

How to Be Happy

Honorable acts breed happiness. We can't lie, cheat, or steal and feel good about ourselves. Low self-worth is the byproduct of deceitful behaviors. Our souls know what's right and what's wrong. God has his fingerprint on us, and when we ignore the divine spark and set out on a lesser course, the end result is unhappiness.

Take It Easy

The cowgirl way teaches us all that no matter what, we have to get up and put one foot in front of the other. Someone has to feed the animals . . . but if that is the best you can do that day, that's okay. Every day doesn't have to be fruitful. No one will judge you, so please, don't judge yourself.

Moods

Animals have moods—at least the fur babies that I've known and loved did—and those moods are authentic to their character. Sure, sometimes animals can have a bad day, but with all the dogs that I've owned and loved and with my horse, I can say that 99 percent of the time, I knew what to expect from them. I could count on them to be consistent—whether it was for them to be snarky, snappy, high-strung, or docile, they were real.

With people, it's different. They can be sneaky. Duplicitous. We can't predict their words or actions. That's why we need to get a grip and conquer *our own* emotions.

If your day is based on what others do or say, you've

not mastered your responses and will be forever driven mad by other people's words or actions. Detach. We can let others have their feelings and their words without allowing their moods or speech to bleed into our day.

Boundaries

Trails have natural boundaries that can impede passage. Some rivers rage wide and deep and cannot be crossed. There are steep mountains with timber so thick even sunlight has to work hard to spread its rays, and there are cliffs so sheer even a donkey would refuse to tread up them.

We accept boundaries in the natural world, so why are we reluctant to set boundaries in our personal lives?

People fear how others will react to their boundaries.

A rancher isn't going to worry about hurting a passing rider's feelings. He's going to do what's best and build fences to keep the cattle contained.

We too are allowed to erect proverbial fences around

our heads and our hearts, without guilt, without fear. It is okay to protect ourselves from emotionally dangerous people who drift too far into our lane and threaten our serenity.

Imperfection

We can have experiences that are profound, yet imperfect—much like the ride that inspired this book. Imperfection is where the learning starts, yet some people struggle to accept themselves and their imperfections.

Perfectionism is birthed in low self-worth and self-esteem. It feeds off of the fear of being judged, of not being good enough. But these beliefs about yourself are false.

Look within to find out where your perfectionism started. Do you practice behaviors that make you feel bad about yourself? Are you a people-pleaser? What negative or traumatic experience from your past still haunts you? Do you believe that if you're perfect, you'll be lovable? Perfectionism is steeped in emotional pain and fibs that you tell yourself. Find the source. Know what's true. Heal the wound.

The Corner of Bitter and Sweet

It's always in hindsight that we can see how a particular event shaped us. God tells us that we will have hardships, yet we continue to think that our lives should be devoid of suffering—that we should be shielded from the bad things that happen. And when suffering gives us a visit, we are angry—we are shaken to the core. Why are we shaken? After all, God told us that life would be hard. He says, "I have told you this so that you might have peace in me. In the world you will have trouble, but take courage, I have conquered the world" (John 16:33).

It took me a long time to understand that God does not cause bad things to happen, yet he is there to help us through. Adversity is not to be feared; if we never had troubles, how would any of us learn to lean on the Lord? How would any of us ever grow up?

Recall the battle that King Jehoshaphat and his people faced. It was Jahaziel, a Levite and the son of Zechariah, who relayed the words of the Lord and reminded the people that they didn't have to fight and bear their load alone:

"You will not have to fight in this encounter. Take your places, and stand firm, and see how the Lord will be with you to deliver you, Judah and Jerusalem. Do not fear or lose heart. Tomorrow go out to meet them, and the Lord will be with you." Then Jehoshaphat knelt down with his face to the ground, and all Judah and the inhabitants of Jerusalem fell down before the Lord in worship (2 Chronicles 20:17–18).

The Lord told them to stand firm and to go out and meet their enemies. The people of Judah must have wondered, *Is he serious?* Yet they obeyed, and they experienced a miracle: "When Judah came to the watchtower of the desert and looked toward the throng, they saw only corpses fallen on the ground, with no survivors" (2 Chronicles 20:24).

How in the world did that happen? The people of Judah didn't have to lift a finger to fight.

God delivered help to the people, and if he did it for them, he will do it for you.

Decide right now that whenever you face a trial, you will go to God first. Decide that you will walk with God on a daily basis and that you will go forth knowing that you're not alone. Keep in mind that in every battle you face, God will be right there with you.

Silence

Are you uncomfortable with silence—that space of infinite nothingness that's devoid of the bookends of noise? Sound provides structure. Do you feel untethered by the lack of noise that defines the seconds, minutes, or hours of the day?

There's security in knowing what comes next. Aha, the rumbling of the school bus—time for the kids to come home. There's the chime of the clock, the din of a television, the hum of the garage door opening, the clang of dishes and silverware when someone fixes a meal.

Stillness causes many to feel untethered as if floating anchorless in a sea of silence. Once you learn to turn within and let go of the sounds that outline your life, you'll become tethered to your own heart.

Anxiety

My palomino, Sham, was anxious. He had a history of abuse, but I knew he could be saved. He needed someone he could trust, and over time, he came to trust me implicitly. When he first became mine, he wanted little to do with people. His first instinct was to flee. He was scared of everything: the bit, the saddle, the barn, the stall, the horse trailer. The only space where he felt okay was in the pasture—probably because it was easy to put distance between himself and humans.

Once I won Sham's trust though, his anxiety—at least in my presence—was nonexistent.

Like horses, when we lack faith and trust in the things and people around us, we can become anxious.

Anxiety is the result of feeling out of control. Anxious people want control because control makes them feel more secure. Perhaps the overwhelming need to feel safe spurs your anxiety. When we project and worry about what may or may not happen, we create inner turmoil, but our lives don't unfold in the future. They unfold right now.

Be where you are. Deal with the people and circumstances that are in front of you. Breathe love into any disharmony. Talk to God. Sing to the Lord: "Give thanks to the Lord, for his mercy endures forever" (2 Chronicles 20:21).

Get out of your own way. Find a God that's bigger than you and bigger than your problems.

The story of Jehoshaphat's battle is a small part of the Bible, but it is big in concept—Jehoshaphat had no other option but to lean on God, and he and his people prevailed.

When we understand that much of our anxiety comes from something in our current situation that we find unacceptable, when we can relinquish control, let go, and give it all to God, we will find peace. "Do not fear or lose heart at the sight of this vast multitude, for the battle is not yours but God's" (2 Chronicles 20:15).

Horse Medicine

With horses, you know where you stand. They're honest like that.

Fight or Flight

Horses are flight animals. When they sense danger, their instinct is to run. With people, it's often the opposite: we know something can be dangerous, but we run toward it: overeating, alcohol, drugs, toxic relationships . . .

Horses are reluctant to step where they don't feel safe. Take a spoonful of horse medicine and think twice before rushing into relationships and situations that might be damaging.

One afternoon, the same week as the cattle drive, I headed out with several of the wranglers. Our job this time was to find and move the cattle from their winter pastures to their spring pastures farther up the mountain. As we moved up the mountain, there were pockets of dense trees. JR wanted nothing to do with the mangled piles of sticks and tree trunks that littered the ground. He refused to step into the timber.

The other horses must have made the same decision because it became a battle of wills for all of the riders. None of the horses wanted to enter the woods, but someone needed to flush out the cow, who stood there staring like we were the silly ones.

You gotta love cowboys, especially those that are good with a lasso. With a few flicks of his wrist, one of the wranglers roped the cow and, in no time, guided it out of the mass of dead trees.

Cows are dumb like that—they'll go where they shouldn't go, and then they get stuck. Isn't that what we do too though? We want what we want, and then we plunge into situations without asking God for guidance, and in no time, we're up to our necks in commotion. We think we have everything under control. We think that we know what we're doing, when the truth is that we don't have a clue.

We could save ourselves all sorts of aggravation and heartache if we got in the habit of asking for guidance *before* we leap. We can't see the whole picture, but God can. Next time, remember to ask God for his blessing and guidance, wait for his answer, and then move forward.

Relationships

Are we going to be takers and trauma makers or agents of encouragement and change? Make a choice. Do you want to sow harmony and peace? Are you the calm or the tempest? Every day we get to choose what we'll bring to the day and to the people in our lives. Choose wisely.

Gear Up

On the trail, we need the right gear. In life we need the right gear too: prayer, humility, acceptance—the sort of gear that endures through time.

Life

Life happens.

Stop manipulating.

Rest.

Breathe.

Let things be.

Trust.

Let go.

Remember that circumstances have a way of working themselves out without your intervention.

Your Goal

Your goal is to be comfortable in your own skin without adjuncts or accolades.

Trust

Trust that when you scatter good seeds, the ones sown in faith will bloom.

Wait and Grow

The story of Jehoshaphat speaks to our desire for instant gratification, yet only in the waiting did King Jehoshaphat see God's miracle. Modern society has made most things so convenient that the art of waiting has been lost.

When I'm waiting for something that I desperately want to happen and I have zero guarantee that it will happen, can I wait with grace? The answer is likely no. Instead of waiting, it's more like, *Let's see what I can do to speed things up.* In essence, the impulse is to force our will because waiting is too hard.

The people of Judah were in a dire predicament. How did they feel after King Jehoshaphat threw himself on the ground, uttered a prayer, and then told them to wait on God? "Then Jehoshaphat knelt down with his face to the ground, and all Judah and the inhabitants of Jerusalem fell down before the Lord in worship" (2 Chronicles 20:18).

The people were forced to wait. Would the king's prayers be answered? No one could say, but what the king did next was even more baffling, for "In the early morning they hastened out to the wilderness of Tekoa. As they were going out, Jehoshaphat halted and said: 'Listen to me, Judah and inhabitants of Jerusalem! Trust in the Lord, your God, and you will be found firm. Trust in his prophets and you will succeed'" (2 Chronicles 20:20).

Then, "after consulting with the people," Jehoshaphat "appointed some to sing to the Lord and some to praise the holy Appearance as it went forth at the head of the army" (2 Chronicles 20:21).

So let's get this straight. While the people are in dire straits and they have armies closing in on them, the king appoints some of his people to sing to the Lord—an action that at the time must have seemed insane and not at all helpful—but here again, what do we know? We think we know what's best, but most times, we actually don't.

Waiting is part of life—life starts out as a nine-month wait—and from there our waits only get longer. What is more important than the wait itself is *how* we wait. Can we get on with life, or are we paralyzed with anguish because we don't know how the story ends?

Nothing grows on the top of the mountain, but there's plenty of growth in the valley. Waiting puts many in a valley of sorts. It is during this visit in the valley that we learn patience and endurance, two attributes that God wants all of us to have.

Take the *Agave americana*, an evergreen perennial that can take decades to bloom. Even when it looks like nothing is happening, the plant is readying itself for the day it will flower. Everything in life unfolds in its own time. Nothing worthwhile happens in a moment.

Can you imagine the perseverance needed to wait years before you get to see what sort of blooms will emerge? There is no substitute for persistence, patience, and grit. Learn to stick with it. If you're doing something that you believe is right but you still haven't received the desired results, don't give up. God wants us to persevere. He wants us to keep the faith, because in waiting, our spirits grow strong.

To Die to Ourselves

To die to our neediness,

To die to our wants and desires,

To die to our resentments, fear, and greed,

To die to our selfishness is when we die to ourselves and learn how to live.

Faith

Those things that scare you are as impermanent and fleeting as shadows.

When you feel scared or stuck, move your feet. Absence of fear should not be your intention; rather, you should acknowledge your fear and move forward anyway. Treat faith like a verb. Action is everything.

Passion

To discover your passion is to discover a power that plants you in the middle of life. Search for that one thing that you can do that allows the time to slip away, that one thing that makes your pulse quicken—is there any better cure for apathy?

Passions are like rocket fuel. They make each day exciting! Regardless of how frivolous others may deem your quest, you owe it to yourself to find something that you can embrace, something that makes you smile, something that keeps you out of your head. A passionate life is a purposeful life—may you find it now.

Honesty

Honesty is not me telling the truth about you. Real honesty is me getting honest with me. The hardest person to be honest with is yourself. Self-honesty requires that we have the maturity and insight to take those hard looks at ourselves, recognize areas for growth, and then implement and practice new behaviors to bring about the desired change.

Each day is a new beginning. Pray for the courage to be vulnerable, to be authentic, to live in a way that resonates with your soul. Your opportunities to evolve are endless and ongoing.

Whirlwinds

Most times, I groomed my horse as he stood cross-tied in the aisle of the barn. When the weather cooperated, I'd open the doors on each end of the walkway to catch the breeze. Every once in a while, out of nowhere, a dust devil took shape. I'd watch the whirlwind travel across the pasture and whoosh into the barn. The mini tornado would kick up a small cloud of dust, and then it'd fizzle out.

Try not to be like the dust devils. Try not to be the sort of person who moves through other people's lives creating a trail of chaos and dust, only to disappear and leave others to clean up the mess.

Pathway to Peace

Develop a relationship with God.

Make a decision to cut noxious people from your life.

Let go of trying to control people, places, and things—it only makes you feel resentful and exhausted. Stop the madness.

Laugh more.

Forgive.

Honor your creativity.

Vow to live a more spiritual life.

Love as many people as much as you can.

Let go of your projected outcomes, and allow situations and life to unfold as they will.

Rein in your expectations, particularly of others.

Loneliness

Horses are herd animals. They do best when they're surrounded by a herd or at least a few other horses. Like horses, people need connections. We want to feel like we belong. As technology develops, we have more and more ways to connect, yet people feel disconnected. Loneliness eats away at the soul, and if you stay lonely too long, you'll come to believe that you're not lovable.

We have an epidemic of loneliness. Why? Is it social media? Fractured families? Addiction? Materialism? The use of technology in lieu of direct contact?

We long for connections, yet it's easier and easier to isolate. No one wants to feel the sting of rejection, but we are not who loves or rejects us. We are spirits living human experiences, and in service to others, we will experience the fullness of connection that drives loneliness away.

Praise God

Remember, King Jehoshaphat and his people were frightened. Yet they didn't let their fear of what-ifs keep them from praising God even before they knew what the outcome of their situation would be.

"After consulting with the people, [Jehoshaphat] appointed some to sing to the Lord and some to praise the holy Appearance as it went forth at the head of the army. They sang, 'Give thanks to the Lord, for his mercy endures forever.' At the moment they began their jubilant hymn, the Lord laid an ambush against the Ammonites, Moabites, and those of Mount Seir who were coming against Judah, so that they were vanquished" (2 Chronicles 20: 21–22).

God answered when King Jehoshaphat's people stepped out in faith. God answered when they acted as if their prayer had already been answered. It is hard for us to move forward in faith when we cannot see the outcome. Some may wonder if God even hears them.

The story of King Jehoshaphat teaches us that we need to pray and move forward in faith while praising God and believing that what we hope and wish for has already been done. The one caveat is that we have to accept that God does not think the way humans think. His answers and solutions often look nothing like we expect them to.

Regardless of our circumstances, King Jehoshaphat encourages us to look toward God. Our circumstances may be nothing like an invasion of armies, but our thoughts can be as destructive as any army, unless we have a cornerstone. Let God be your rock. Give him your life.

Onward

If we try to move forward while looking back over our shoulders, we're bound to stumble. Look ahead, for your future lies there.

Pay Attention

Awareness is the key. You can't change the things you don't like about yourself until you become aware of them.

Little growth comes if you slam your mind shut and refuse to consider the "maybe." Are there things in your life and in your behavior that no longer serve you well? Are you ready to look within?

Changing the past is impossible, but we can change any objectionable behaviors so that our future will not resemble our past.

Most people change, but not that much—unless some crisis forces the change. Others change when they are graced with clarity, but even then, without the willingness to be different and do different, the change will be slight.

Today, I will stay open. I'll be willing to change the things about myself that need to be changed.

Humility

Humility means being confident enough to say, "I don't know," or, "Perhaps you're right."

Humility allows others to have the last word.

Like King Jehoshaphat, we need to rely on God and not on our egos.

An overinflated ego convinces us to do things that we're not meant to do or to move in directions that we're not meant to go. Get your ego out of the way, and wait on the Lord.

Ripples

You are significant.
Your life matters.
Your voice matters.
Your presence here on this earth matters.
Believe that you can make a positive impact in someone else's life. You cannot see or know all the ripples you've created, but rest assured, your influence is felt.

Half of the Sky

Next time you judge someone, remember that from wherever you live in the world, you only get to see half of the sky.

Approval and Validation

If you had two water troughs in the pasture but one was always dry, the animals would figure it out. They'd stop going to the dry trough to get a drink of water.

If an animal can figure out that it can't get water from a dry well, we too can stop looking for validation and approval from people who are dry wells.

You'd never shop for a birthday cake at the tack store, so decide right now that you'll no longer seek validation or approval from people who are incapable of providing emotional love and support. Instead, look to God. He has an unlimited amount of love, grace, and joy to give, and his well will never run dry.

Note to Reader

Dear reader, we've tackled a few mountains together, and now we've come to the end of the trail. As you journeyed through the pages, I pray that you took time to pause and reflect. It's my sincerest wish that by now you've come to understand that if you want peace in your life, aspire to be more like King Jehoshaphat. He found a faith that worked for him in the direst of circumstances. What if we could have that sort of faith under all conditions? How much less stress would we feel? How much more peaceful would our daily lives be?

By now you've come to understand how fretting over outcomes and manipulating situations and perceptions are destructive actions that sap your energy and steal your joy.

We live from the inside out, but the world lives from the outside in. Letting go allows you to feel better. When you let go, the stress of what might happen is no longer your concern. When we live faith-filled lives, we experience less stress, anxiety, and fear. Are you ready to let go?

The following questions and prompts will help you heal and let go. To get the maximum benefit, please write out your answers.

What would your life look like if you no longer cared what other people thought? What would that sort of freedom look like?

Who do you need to forgive? What do you gain by harboring any resentment.

List your top five fears. Can you picture yourself letting go of them and placing them in God's hands? How does holding on to those fears impact your life?

Consider your anger (be brutally honest here). What do you get out of massaging your anger? What might it feel like to let go and live free instead?

Now that you've looked at what's blocking you, I suggest that you take your written responses and burn them up in the fireplace or a safe place outdoors. This will be a symbolic gesture that will provide a distinct visual of what it means to let go so that you may move forward and live your best life.

For particularly difficult problems and people that steal your serenity, here's a plan:

For the next thirty days (or sixty, if need be), pray the prayer of King Jehoshaphat, and read Psalms 55 and 56. Your situation may not change, but your heart and your perspective *will* change, and you will finally be able to live in peace, or God will give you the courage you need to make permanent changes that will bring you peace.

The entire prayer of King Jehoshaphat can be found in verses 6–12 of 2 Chronicles 20. I like the shortened version of the prayer (2 Chronicles 20:6) because it's easy to memorize and the last sentence is gold: "Lord, God of our fathers, are you not the God in heaven, and do you not rule over all the kingdoms of the nations? In your hand is power and might, and no one can withstand you."

Pray. Trust. Ride.

Readers, I want to hear from you. Please let me know how the prayer of King Jehoshaphat and letting go has changed your life! You may contact me at: info@Lisaboucherauthor.com

Appendix:

Who Was King Jehoshaphat?

By Pastor Michelle Terry

King Jehoshaphat was the fourth ruler of the Kingdom of Judah, from 870–846 BCE. After the death of Solomon, Ancient Israel split into two kingdoms, with the northern territory remaining the Kingdom of Israel and the southern territory becoming the Kingdom of Judah. Jehoshaphat succeeded his father, Asa, and was succeeded by his son, Jehoram.

Overall, Scripture portrays Jehoshaphat as a good ruler. He is mentioned in both 1 Kings and 2 Chronicles, but 2 Chronicles gives significantly more detail about his reign than 1 Kings. In both, Jehoshaphat is credited with insisting Ahab, king of Israel, consult with the prophet Micaiah before the battle against Ramoth-Gilead.

In 2 Chronicles, Jehoshaphat is credited with wide-spanning reforms in Judah. In addition to fortifying the cities he ruled (2 Chronicles 17:2),[**] Jehoshaphat made a number of religious reforms. He removed "high places and sacred poles" from Judah (2 Chronicles 17:6), meaning he stopped the worship of other gods in Judah. (Though, interestingly, they would return before his reign was over, as noted in 2 Chronicles 20:33). He also sent Levites and priests to the cities of Judah to teach the citizens God's law (2 Chronicles 17:7).

Since he was so faithful to God, neighboring kingdoms around Judah respected King Jehoshaphat. They did not wage war against Judah and instead brought gifts and riches as tribute (2 Chronicles 17:10–12). Jehoshaphat built a great military presence, and the Kingdom of Judah was strong (2 Chronicles 17:13–19).

Though the alliance with King Ahab was considered a mistake in 2 Chronicles, Jehoshaphat survived

---

* The scriptural references in this appendix are from page 531 of the New Oxford Annotated Bible with the Apocryphal/Deuterocanonical Books, New Revised Standard Version, edited by Michael D. Coogan and published in New York by Oxford University Press in 2001.

the battle and is credited for having the will to seek the Lord (2 Chronicles 19:4). He returned to Jerusalem and established a new judicial system, in which he appointed judges in every city and told them to consider themselves judges on the Lord's behalf (2 Chronicles 19:5–6).

In the time following those reforms, word arrived from messengers that Judah would be attacked by "a great multitude." Jehoshaphat recognized that Judah was outnumbered and turned the battle over to God. He let go of the outcome and prayed for God to help them. The prophet Jahaziel, visited by God's spirit, told the people of Judah that they should not fight. Everyone worshipped God that evening, and the next day they sang and worshipped as the battle began. The enemies destroyed one another without Judah joining the battle (2 Chronicles 20:1–24).

Jehoshaphat's focus on God and faithfulness to God's word led to a prosperous reign. Though he occasionally made mistakes, he constantly kept his focus on God. As a result, Judah flourished and Jehoshaphat was given honor both from Judah's inhabitants and surrounding lands.

Acknowledgments

A special thank-you to Melinda Eubel, the best beta reader a girl could have. Thank you for your time and, mostly, your eagle eye. You don't miss a thing! I'd also like to give a shout-out to my friend Mary Ryan Wineberg, who I learned loves words as much as I do and who was a great help in nailing down the title! And, as always, thank you to everyone at She Writes Press who takes our words and makes them into books. I appreciate everything you all do.

Credits

About the Author

photo credit: Katie Swift Photography

Lisa Boucher is the award-winning author of *Raising The Bottom: Making Mindful Choices in a Drinking Culture*. She has contributed to notable publications such as *Shape Magazine* and *U.S. News & World Report* and is a frequent guest on numerous syndicated radio and podcast shows. She is highly intuitive and has assisted hundreds of people in healing from substance abuse, depression, and anxiety. A registered nurse, Lisa believes having a strong spiritual connection with God, helps us surrender the things in our lives that we cannot control. She's married and is the mother of twins.

SELECTED TITLES FROM SHE WRITES PRESS

She Writes Press is an independent publishing company founded to serve women writers everywhere. Visit us at www.shewritespress.com.

Raising the Bottom: Making Mindful Choices in a Drinking Culture by Lisa Boucher. $16.95, 978-1-63152-214-7
Women share their drinking stories of hitting rock bottom—so you don't ever have to.

Beyond Jesus: My Spiritual Odyssey by Patricia A. Pearce
$16.95, 978-1-63152-359-5
In the crucible of grief following a friend's death, Patricia Pearce resolved to open herself to hidden dimensions of her existence—not realizing her quest would cost her her vocation as a Presbyterian pastor, open her eyes to the radical implications of Jesus's message, and uncover what she believes is the key to our spiritual evolution.

Finding Venerable Mother: A Daughter's Spiritual Quest to Thailand by Cindy Rasicot. $16.95, 978-1-63152-702-9
In midlife, Cindy travels halfway around the world to Thailand and unexpectedly discovers a Thai Buddhist nun who offers her the unconditional love and acceptance her own mother was never able to provide. This soulful and engaging memoir reminds readers that when we go forward with a truly open heart, faith, forgiveness, and love are all possible.

Hidden Treasure: How to Break Free of Five Patterns that Hide Your True Self by Alice McDowell, PhD. $16.95, 978-1-63152-586-304-5
An inspiring, illuminating book that examines five personality patterns—called character structures—and teaches you how to break free of these patterns through effective exercises, compelling true stories, fun cartoons, and spiritual insights so you can live a freer, more radiant life.